# FALCONS

# LIVING WILD

Published by Creative Education and Creative Paperbacks
P.O. Box 227, Mankato, Minnesota 56002
Creative Education and Creative Paperbacks are imprints of The Creative Company
www.thecreativecompany.us

Design and production by Mary Herrmann
Art direction by Rita Marshall
Printed in Malaysia

Photographs by Corbis (68/Ocean, Eric and David Hosking, Sebastian Kennerknecht/
Minden Pictures, Louie Psihoyos, Michael Quinton/Minden Pictures, Ruaridh Stewart/
ZUMA Press, JULIAN STRATENSCHULTE/epa, Sandro Vannini), Creative Commons
Wikimedia (Aviceda, Hector Bottai, Bohuš Číčel, Marc Dalmulder, Chris Eason, Greg
Hume, Dennis Jarvis, Maureen Leong-Kee, Sumeet Moghe, Artur Nowak, Tony Wills),
Dreamstime (Neil Harrison, Kc Ci), Shutterstock (Inna Astakhova, Andrew Astbury,
Bildagentur Zoonar GmbH, chbaum, CnOPhoto, Linn Currie, CyberKat, Rusty Dodson,
Dennis Donohue, Richard Fitzer, Chris Hill, Jearu, jurra8, kospet, Geoffrey Kuchera,
MarclSchauer, Johannes Dag Mayer, Paul Reeves Photography, Styve Reineck, Sue
Robinson, rook76, Porojnicu Stelian, Txanbelin, uhueye, Vishnevskiy Vasily), WikiArt
(Aubrey Beardsley)

Library of Congress Cataloging-in-Publication Data
Gish, Melissa.
Falcons / Melissa Gish.
p. cm. — (Living wild)
Includes bibliographical references and index.
Summary: A look at falcons, including their habitats, physical characteristics such as their
wings, behaviors, relationships with humans, and their threatened status in the world today.
ISBN 978-1-60818-566-5 (hardcover)
ISBN 978-1-62832-167-8 (pbk)
1. Falcons—Juvenile literature. 2. Rare birds—Juvenile literature. I. Title.

QL696.F34G57 2015
598.9'6—dc23    2014028009

CCSS: RI.5.1, 2, 3, 8; RST.6-8.1, 2, 5, 6, 8; RH.6-8.3, 4, 5, 6, 7, 8

First Edition HC 9 8 7 6 5 4 3 2 1
First Edition PBK 9 8 7 6 5 4 3 2 1

**CREATIVE EDUCATION • CREATIVE PAPERBACKS**

# FALCONS

Melissa Gish

In the lush, windswept prairie of Wyoming's Thunder Basin National Grassland, an American kestrel

sits atop a telephone pole, watching a deer
mouse climb a thick stalk of western wheatgrass.

**T**he lush, windswept prairie of Wyoming's Thunder Basin National Grassland spans more than a half million acres (202,343 ha) between the Big Horn Mountains and the Black Hills. Here, a kestrel—North America's smallest falcon—sits atop a telephone pole, watching a deer mouse climb a thick stalk of western wheatgrass. The mouse climbs to the top of the stalk and begins munching the seeds.

It does not notice the bird eyeing its every move. The kestrel chooses this moment to strike. With a bob of its head and tail, the kestrel launches from the pole. Its wings tucked tightly against its body, the hungry bird dives toward the mouse. With a sudden upturn, it spreads its wings like sails. Catching the wind, the falcon angles sideways in midair. It digs its claws into the mouse's soft body, plucking it from the grass, and flaps its wings again, lifting its prey skyward.

# WHERE IN THE WORLD THEY LIVE

■ **Peregrine Falcon**
Americas, Asia, and Australia

■ **Amur Falcon**
eastern Asia

■ **African Hobby**
East Africa

■ **Australian Hobby**
throughout Australia

■ **Saker Falcon**
eastern Europe and central Asia

■ **Gyrfalcon**
Arctic regions of Asia, Europe, and North America

■ **Laggar Falcon**
Middle East and southern Asia

■ **American Kestrel**
United States, Mexico, and South America

True falcons comprise 39 species that inhabit nearly every continent and a variety of environments, from forests to deserts to urban areas. Some falcons migrate thousands of miles each year, and species such as the peregrine falcon contain numerous subspecies. The colored squares represent some of the areas in which eight falcon species can be found.

## OUR FASTEST FLIERS

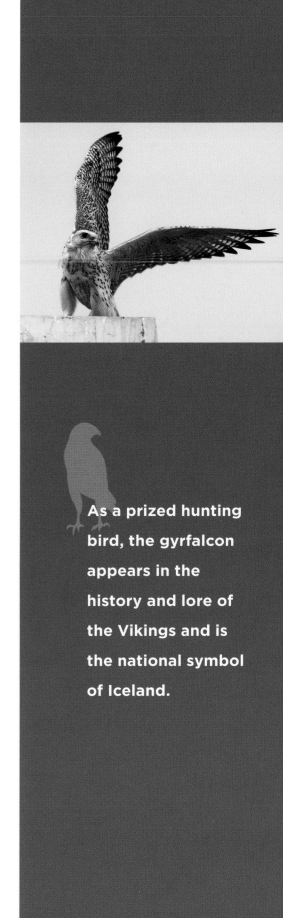

As members of the order Falconiformes, falcons and their relatives—eagles, hawks, and vultures—are raptors, or birds of prey. About 60 falcons, caracaras, and forest falcons make up the Falconidae family. Unlike other raptors, they use their beaks rather than their feet to kill prey. More than 35 species of Falconidae are true falcons, including hobbies and kestrels. These birds inhabit every continent on Earth except Antarctica.

The name "falcon" stems from the Latin *falx*, which means "curved blade." This word probably referred to the bird's sharply curved beak or feet. Later on, *faucon* was used in France and England as the name for birds of prey active during the daytime. Falcons are known for their swift flight and dazzling aerial acrobatics. Their wing feathers can be as much as three times the length of their wing bones. The narrow, tapered wings of falcons give them the unique ability to fly at high speeds and maneuver sharply.

The largest falcon is the gyrfalcon (*JER-fal-kin*), a bird that lives in Arctic and subarctic habitats around the world. As with many birds, female falcons are typically 10 to 20 percent larger than males. A female gyrfalcon's

**As a prized hunting bird, the gyrfalcon appears in the history and lore of the Vikings and is the national symbol of Iceland.**

*Most of the 800-some Seychelles kestrels are found on Mahé, the largest island of the group.*

wingspan may be more than five feet (1.5 m), and their bodies are two feet (0.6 m) long from head to tail. They typically weigh less than five pounds (2.3 kg), though, thanks to the hollow bone structure shared by all birds. The smallest falcon in the world is the Seychelles kestrel. Averaging 7 inches (17.8 cm) in length with a 16-inch (40.6 cm) wingspan, this bird generally weighs no more than 3 ounces (85 g). The Seychelles kestrel is found in small numbers on fewer than 10 of the 116 Seychelles Islands northeast of Madagascar, where it is the only nesting bird of prey. People who speak Seychellois Creole, a language on the islands, call this bird *katiti*.

The fastest land animal is the cheetah, and the fastest sea creature is the sailfish. Both are able to travel 70 miles (113 km) per hour, but neither would be able to beat the peregrine falcon in a race. The fastest animal on the planet, the peregrine falcon can travel 200 miles (322 km) per hour while diving through the sky. The peregrine falcon is also the most widespread raptor in the world. Its 19 subspecies are found in nearly every habitat except Earth's coldest regions and wettest tropical rainforests. Because of its vast range, the peregrine falcon enjoys

Scientists have cataloged 19 peregrine falcon subspecies according to the birds' geographical locations.

*Saker falcons are determined hunters, patiently waiting for their prey to emerge before swooping for the kill.*

relative stability in its population. Other falcons are not so fortunate. The Réunion kestrel, named for its small island home east of Madagascar, was overhunted to **extinction** by 17th-century French settlers.

Throughout history, humans have viewed falcons as pests, captured them for food or sport, or driven them from their habitats through land development. Yet most falcon species have managed to survive and even thrive because of their **adaptability**. The lesser kestrel, whose population had plummeted in western Europe by the middle of the 20th century, is now abundant throughout a variety of habitats from South Africa to northern Europe. Likewise, the Australian hobby inhabits much of the continent, from open grasslands to woodlands and dense forests. The saker falcon, though endangered, is able to survive in Europe's foothills and mountains, the deserts of the Arabian Peninsula, and the Asian **steppes**.

As birds, falcons are **warm-blooded**, feathered, beaked animals that walk on two feet and lay eggs. Like other birds of prey, they search for food using their powerful eyesight and have strong, hooked beaks and razor-like talons on each toe to tear apart flesh. Falcons are

Lesser kestrels fly 1,740 miles (2,800 km) annually to Senegal, where they feast on the plentiful locusts.

**Often targeted for the falconry trade in the Middle East and Asia, saker falcons are now threatened with extinction.**

*Falcons have special flaps in their nares, or nostrils, to regulate their breathing while flying through the air.*

**Male falcons are called tiercels ("thirds") for the ancient belief that every third falcon egg contained a male.**

sometimes confused with hawks, and while they often look similar, their hunting tactics set them apart. Hawks typically swoop down from a perch and land on their victims with crushing weight and talons that stab prey to death. Unlike hawks, falcons use their beaks to kill prey after it has been captured. Falcons lack teeth and must land or perch to eat. They shred their meals, swallowing the meat as well as feathers, fur, bones, claws, teeth, insect shells—everything. The indigestible bits of food are vomited up several hours after a meal in the form of small, round or oblong masses called pellets. All raptors cast out pellets almost daily.

The falcon's beak is made of keratin, the same material found in human fingernails. A notch in the upper beak called a tomial tooth slices into a prey animal's neck and severs the spinal cord. Some falcon species use their beaks to nab birds or bats out of the air. Others feed on ground-dwelling prey, such as voles, mice, and squirrels. Small falcons, such as the American kestrel, eat mice, lizards, scorpions, and large insects. The falcon's closest relatives are the roughly 10 species of caracara. These large birds share the falcon's characteristic beak. However, because

A 2014 study found that peregrine falcons hunt other birds by predicting the flight path of their prey.

*Once their prey is in sight, kestrels bob their heads several times before diving down to attack.*

they are slow fliers, caracaras scavenge **carrion** rather than actively hunt. They are found in the southwestern United States, Mexico, and Central and South America.

To locate prey, falcons rely on their powerful vision, which is at least twice as strong as a human's. A falcon's eyes, located on the side of the skull, look outward and forward at the same time. This is called binocular vision, and it helps falcons judge distances precisely. Protection from dust and direct sunlight is provided by a nictitating (*NIK-tih-tayt-ing*) membrane (a see-through inner eyelid) that closes from front to back. In addition, two sets of **glands** similar to human tear ducts produce an oily substance that keeps the eyes moist, which is especially useful when falcons fly at high speeds.

Falcons have powerful wings. As juveniles, falcons have extra long wing feathers that allow them to practice maneuvering in flight. As they grow older, falcons lose these wing feathers in a process called molting and grow new feathers that are narrower and tapered. With little wind resistance, falcons can fly fast and turn sharply without losing speed, allowing them to easily overtake prey in flight.

The laggar falcon is slower than most falcons but flies with the sun behind it—in effect, hiding from its prey.

*As part of the courtship ritual, a male and female falcon may gently tap each other's beak.*

## FABULOUS FALCONS

Most species of falcon can live up to 15 years in the wild or up to 25 years in captivity. Falcons reach maturity and are ready to mate at about two years old. To begin the mating process, a male falcon will select a nest site and then perform a series of aerial acrobatics called flight displays. High-speed swooping and diving are meant to attract the attention of females. For about a month, females watch these displays. A male will also call to the females and bring them food to encourage them to follow him to his selected nest site. Uninterested females move on to watch other males. Females considering the persistent male must decide if he demonstrates acceptable strength and agility—necessary characteristics for successful parenting. The first female to accept a male becomes his mate. Most falcon species return year after year to the same place to mate with the same partner. However, if one dies, the other will find a new mate.

At the nest site—usually a ledge on a cliff or in a cave—the male continues to perform for his partner. He raises his tail and bows his head while staring at the female and vocalizing. Soon she joins him in bowing and

*Male falcons performing courtship flight displays often swoop over potential nest sites.*

**Mated pairs of many falcon species hunt and feed cooperatively, with the male locating prey for the female to capture.**

*Kestrel nestlings ensure the feeding area stays clean by keeping their waste to the outer edges of the nest.*

vocalizing. Then they set to work creating their nest. Unlike many other birds that gather materials to build a nest, falcons simply scrape a depression out of the dirt and leaves on a ledge. This nest-making behavior secures the bond between two falcons. Because of the way they are made, falcon nests are called scrapes.

Most female falcons lay three to five eggs at a rate of one egg per day. The eggs are about two inches (5.1 cm) long, speckled, and vary in color from pink to brown. A group of eggs is called a clutch. Like all birds' eggs, falcon eggs must be incubated, or kept warm, while the baby falcons, called eyases, are developing inside. The female spends the most time incubating the eggs, keeping them tucked under her breast and wings and turning them daily. Throughout the nesting period, the male falcon brings food to his partner. She steps away from the nest to eat, which helps keep the nest clean. Falcons incubate their eggs for 30 to 40 days, and then the eyases hatch.

An eyas chips through the hard shell of its egg with its egg tooth, a sharp projection on the tip of its beak that is later resorbed into the beak. This may take several hours. The eyas emerges wet, but soon its covering of silky gray feathers, called down, dries and becomes a thick, fluffy coat. Newly hatched peregrine falcons weigh about 1.5 ounces (42.5 g). Smaller falcon species weigh about half as much, and larger falcons, such as gyrfalcons, can weigh up to twice that amount. For the first two weeks of their lives, hatchlings depend on their father to bring food to the nest and their mother to tear it into small pieces for them. Falcons often fight over food, and in many cases, the strongest falcon eyases will kill the weakest sibling in a practice called siblicide. This behavior improves the chances that the remaining falcons will get enough to eat.

*Falcons must maintain good nutrition in order to lay eggs with shells thick enough to protect the hatchlings.*

*Red-footed falcon eyases will soon weigh 5.5 ounces (156 g) and have wingspans of 26 to 30 inches (66–76.2 cm).*

**The Madagascar kestrel's adaptive abilities in both wilderness and urban areas make it the island's most common raptor.**

At about two weeks of age, the eyases can be left alone—sometimes all day—as both parents hunt for food. The parents bring prey to the nest and allow the eyases to tear it apart themselves. This helps the young birds develop the use of their beaks and talons. Falcons are some of the fastest-growing birds in the world. Over the next two to three weeks, the young falcons lose their fluffy down in favor of new feathers. Now called fledglings, they have flight feathers longer than those of their parents. Learning to perform the acrobatics for which falcons are well known takes practice, and longer flight feathers allow young falcons to conserve energy as they learn to fly.

Fledglings leave the nest to explore their surroundings and to begin hunting on their own. However, because they are inexperienced hunters, they typically return to the nest site for two to three more weeks to get food from their parents and roost among their siblings at night. In cold climates, where winters can be harsh and food scarce, upwards of 40 percent of young falcons, called juveniles, fail to survive their first year. In warmer climates, the chances are much better.

Because common kestrels naturally nest in holes in cliffs, they may also nest in building crevices.

Depending on the species, juveniles may not yet have
adult **plumage**. The young of many species, such as
peregrine falcons, have darker markings than adults. The
markings help them to blend in with their surroundings
as they try to avoid predators and to remain hidden from
the eyes of their prey.

As the predator of small prey, a falcon helps maintain
a healthy environment for all the living things in its
habitat by preventing insects and rodents from becoming
overabundant. Farmers especially enjoy seeing falcons

in the sky. The small Amur falcon breeds in Siberia and China and winters in South Africa, and the African hobby lives year round in East Africa. These two species feed on grasshoppers and locusts, which, if left unchecked, can destroy crops. The laughing falcon, named for its loud call, hunts venomous snakes in Mexico and Central and South America, which benefits humans who live in areas where such creatures pose a threat. Many falcon species even make their homes in barns, feeding on mice and rats.

Adult falcons have few natural enemies other than larger birds of prey such as red-shouldered and Cooper's hawks. Humans have the greatest influence on falcon populations around the world. Destroying falcon habitat and shooting, trapping, and poisoning falcons are practices that have reduced the numbers of many falcon species—including the Mauritius kestrel, the grey falcon of Australia, and the Seychelles kestrel. All three have been listed as vulnerable on the Red List of Threatened Species that is published annually by the International Union for Conservation of Nature (IUCN). Because these birds exist in isolated habitats, they could eventually become extinct, if threats continue to be ignored.

*Each year, Amur falcons undertake one of the longest journeys of any bird—flying 13,670 miles (22,000 km).*

**African hobbies flock together to feed on winged termites that come out of their nests after the first heavy rain.**

Images of the falcon god Horus adorn the ancient Egyptian temple at Edfu, built in his honor between 237 and 57 B.C.

## FAST AND FURIOUS

Throughout history, falcons have been associated with the power to travel between the human and spirit worlds. In ancient Egypt, falcons were considered royal birds. The Egyptian god Horus is depicted as having a human body and a falcon's head. Egyptians believed his right eye was the sun and his left eye was the moon. The sun and moon rose and set as Horus traveled across the sky. Horus's right eye was believed to give him the power to see into the future, and it became a symbol of protection and health. The symbol was later adopted by the Romans and Greeks, who called it the *wedjat* and used it as an image of protection.

In Norse **mythology**, Freya is a daughter of Njord, the god of wind and sea. She wears a cloak made of falcon feathers and can turn herself into a falcon at will. She flies over the battlefield and watches over the men. When warriors die in battle, their spirits travel to Asgard—the home of the gods. Half of the dead go to Valhalla, the hall of Odin (ruler of the gods). The rest go to Sessrumnir, the hall of Freya. In Norse tradition, dying in battle is the noblest way to die because it assures an afterlife in the halls of Asgard.

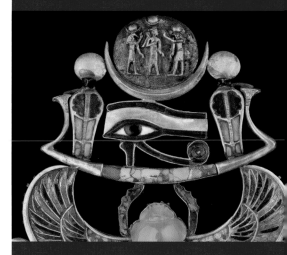

*The wedjat eye can be found on many artifacts of ancient Egypt, including ornate necklaces known as pectorals.*

**Dickinson's kestrel of East Africa is attracted to grass fires because the fleeing mice, lizards, and grasshoppers make easy meals.**

MERLIN TAKETH THE CHILD ARTHVR INTO HIS KEEPING

The wizard Merlin, a character in the tales of King Arthur, was named after the popular bird of medieval falconry.

The falcon is perhaps the most important symbol in the **cultural** history of Hungary. Turul, depicted as an enormous saker falcon, is believed to be the mystical ancestor of all Hungarian people. According to legend, more than 1,000 years ago, Turul, a magical falcon, visited the dreams of Princess Emese. Afterward, she gave birth to a son, whom she named Álmos, meaning "the dreamt one." Turul told Emese that her son would be the father of a great nation—and he was, for he is considered the leader of the first Hungarian tribes. Another story tells how Turul appeared in the dreams of one of Attila's descendants, prompting him to lead his people to the land that ultimately became Hungary.

Today, Hungarian culture embraces Turul the falcon as a symbol of strength and nobility. Turul appears on the **coat of arms** of both the Hungarian army and the national security office. Statues in his likeness can be found throughout Hungary. Two of the most famous Turul statues are located at the gates of Buda Castle in Budapest and at the top of Gerecse Mountain. The latter is the largest bird statue in Europe at nearly 50 feet (15.2 m) wide.

About 2000 B.C., people in ancient China began training falcons to hunt smaller birds for food. This activity, called falconry, made its way from China to the Middle East around 1700 B.C. and then to Europe by the 700s A.D. By the 1600s, falconry had become a royal sport in Europe. A person's social rank determined the size of his bird. Only the king could hunt with a gyrfalcon. Royal servants could hunt with nothing larger than a kestrel. When firearms changed the way people hunted in the 1800s, the popularity of falconry faded. However, it found a new audience in America a

*Gerecse Mountain's famous Turul monument was built in 1907 as a memorial to a Hungarian military victory.*

# GERMAN LOVE SONG

It has pained me in the heart,
Full many a time,
That I yearned after that
Which I may not have,
Nor ever shall win.
It is very grievous.
I do not mean gold or silver;
It is more like a human heart.

I trained me a falcon,
More than a year.
When I had tamed him,
As I would have him,
And had well tied his feathers
With golden chains,
He soared up very high,
And flew into other lands.

I saw the falcon since,
Flying happily;
He carried on his foot
Silken straps,
And his plumage was
All red of gold . . .
May God send them together,
Who would fain be loved.

*excerpt from* Chips from a German Workshop, *by Friedrich Max Müller (1823–1900)*

century later. Today, thousands of people are members of the North American Falconers Association.

Training a falcon takes hard work and dedication, and falcon trainers, called falconers, must work with their birds every day. Young falcons may be taken from a nest in the wild or bred in captivity. A training falcon captured as an eyas keeps this name until it reaches one year old. A training falcon captured during its first year in the wild is a passager, while a training falcon captured as an adult is a haggard. Captive birds wear a leather strap, called a jess, tied to each leg. The falconer holds the jesses between the thumb and forefinger as the bird perches on the hunter's leather-gloved hand. Keeping control of the falcon in this way is called handling the bird. The birds also wear a soft leather hood to keep them calm. When the hunter removes the hood and lets go of the straps, the falcon heads for the sky and immediately sights its prey. While birds do not typically retrieve prey for their masters, they do kill it and hold it on a platform or on the ground until the hunter can retrieve it.

The speed and strength of falcons have made them popular symbols on coins, currency, and stamps around

*Unlike pets, falcons do not bond with or feel affection for falconers; they simply learn to work for rewards.*

**The Barbary falcon, commonly found from northern Africa to Pakistan, does not migrate as many of its relatives do.**

the world. A Barbary falcon appears on Palestine's 10 Qirsh coin, and a peregrine falcon is featured on the Idaho quarter, issued in 2007 by the U.S. Mint as part of the 50 State Quarters series. The New Zealand falcon, that country's only **endemic** bird of prey, is on the New Zealand $20 note. Dozens of falcons appear on postage stamps from Afghanistan to Zimbabwe. Even a fictional falcon appeared on a stamp in 2007. As part of its tribute to the Star Wars film franchise, the U.S. Postal Service included the *Millennium Falcon*—a spaceship named for its super speed—in its commemorative stamp collection. Some real-life vehicles are named for the gravity-defying birds as well. In 1976, the U.S. Air Force began flying the F-16 Fighting Falcon. Since then, more than 20 countries have ordered versions of the F-16 for their air forces. In the 1960s, French aircraft manufacturer Dassault Aviation launched its Falcon series of private jets. Today, some models sell for $45 million.

Falcons also represent a variety of sports teams, such as the Air Force Academy Falcons, who play home football games in Falcon Stadium in Colorado Springs, Colorado. Their team name was selected by the class of

1959, and their mascot, known simply as "The Bird," has remained a fixture for Falcons fans. At Bowling Green State University in Ohio, Freddie and Frieda Falcon are the team's mascots. Fans of the National Football League's Atlanta Falcons have followed the team since 1966. Boasting a number of division championships, the team made its first Super Bowl appearance during the 1998 season.

Star Wars *creator George Lucas once revealed that a hamburger inspired the shape of the* Millennium Falcon.

Scientists believe that the Archaeopteryx grew to the size of a raven, with three claws on its wings.

L ike all birds, falcons **evolved** from hollow-boned reptiles that existed millions of years ago. The link between reptiles and birds is thought to be the *Archaeopteryx*. Remains of this creature with feathered wings and reptilian teeth have been found in southern Germany. It died out with the dinosaurs about 65 million years ago, but other birdlike creatures continued to evolve. Fossils indicate that the first raptors appeared about 50 million years ago. Most falcon ancestors existed in Europe, Asia, and northern Africa. Many modern falcons are found in the same locations they inhabited millions of years ago. The Eurasian hobby, merlin, lesser kestrel, and red-footed falcon are all examples of falcons descended from earlier bird species that lived in prehistoric Europe and the Middle East.

Sometime around 5 or 4 million years ago, falcon ancestors moved from Europe and Asia to North America and diversified. Fossils of prehistoric falcons discovered in Kansas point to similarities with modern merlins. However, these ancient birds were probably smaller with larger feet. Such information has proven valuable to

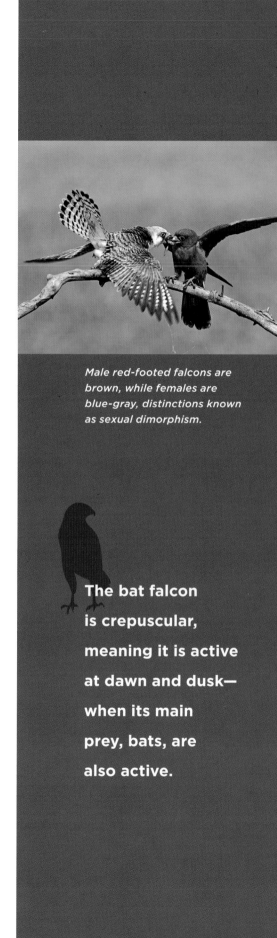

*Male red-footed falcons are brown, while females are blue-gray, distinctions known as sexual dimorphism.*

**The bat falcon is crepuscular, meaning it is active at dawn and dusk— when its main prey, bats, are also active.**

*A 1938 stamp from Czechoslovakia (now the Czech Republic) depicts a peregrine falcon in its mountain habitat.*

scientists who once believed that all falcon ancestors were as large as some of the largest modern species. Another fossil discovery made in Bulgaria in 1990 revealed that one older, smaller falcon ancestor—a kestrel-sized bird called *Falco bakalovi*—existed several million years before the larger falcons evolved.

Many falcon species are abundant today. Despite being nearly wiped out in the 1960s by the effects of chemicals used in agriculture, the peregrine falcon now exists in stable numbers on every continent except Antarctica. Its success story is largely thanks to the banning of the chemical **DDT**, along with serious species recovery efforts over the span of several decades. Sustained research and conservation programs help peregrine falcon populations remain balanced. Other species are not so fortunate. One of the smallest and most rarely seen falcons, the taita falcon is found only in Kenya and surrounding areas, where it survives by eating smaller birds. Pesticide-spraying is the taita's main threat. Worldwide, human activities are the greatest cause of shrinking falcon populations. Falcons suffer from electrocution on power lines and transformers; collisions with windows of tall

buildings and objects such as wind **turbines** and radio towers; and eating **contaminated** prey. Most falcons, though, simply die out when their habitats are destroyed.

In New Zealand, the spread of nonnative animals has caused the New Zealand falcon, also called the karearea, to become one of the country's most endangered birds. **Feral** cats, hedgehogs, pigs, and goats raid falcon nests, devouring eggs and chicks. The Marlborough Falcon Conservation Trust, founded in 2008 to increase awareness of the need to protect the New Zealand falcon,

*Habitat loss has driven many New Zealand falcons to the island nation's elevated region known as "high country."*

*In many states, conservation organizations offer free online instructions for building kestrel nest boxes.*

has reported that fewer than 3,000 New Zealand falcon pairs still exist on the planet.

Humans are the most devastating predator of the Amur falcon, which migrates annually from Siberia to Somalia, Kenya, and South Africa. Along the way, the birds stop to rest in the northeastern India state of Nagaland. It is there that local people, using enormous nets, trap the birds to be sold as food. The wildlife conservation group Conservation India is currently working with the Nagaland state government and the Nagaland Wildlife & Biodiversity

Conservation Trust to end the annual slaughter of an estimated 120,000 to 140,000 falcons. If efforts to protect these migrating birds in India are not successful, the Amur falcon could face an uncertain future.

The American kestrel is a bird that has long felt the pressure of human interference, from habitat loss to chemical contamination of the mice and insects it eats. These birds exist throughout North America. However, their numbers are inconsistent. Researchers believe that the loss of nesting habitat is a major factor in the birds' struggle for survival. Kestrels are secondary cavity nesters, meaning they do not make holes in trees but rather nest inside natural crevices or abandoned holes. As forested land is destroyed to make way for urban development and agriculture, kestrels have access to fewer suitable nest sites.

To assist kestrels, biologists in many states from coast to coast have successfully operated kestrel nest box projects designed to encourage kestrel nesting. Nest boxes are placed in safe areas and then monitored. Sometimes the birds are banded for population studies. Banding is a process by which birds' legs are fitted with a metal or plastic bracelet, called a band. Some bands are colored,

*Australia's brown falcon often hunts like a hawk, patiently waiting on a perch for prey and then dropping onto it.*

**To increase orange-breasted falcon numbers, conservationists breed the birds in Wyoming and release them in Belize.**

and some are imprinted with a number or code. Over months or years, the birds are either viewed using binoculars or temporarily captured and identified by their bands. This method of gathering data works well to count birds and to track those that reuse particular nest boxes. Connecticut's American Kestrel Nest Box Project began in 1978 and has helped increase kestrel populations in the state. Nevertheless, Connecticut still lists the bird as a threatened species. In New Jersey, which classifies kestrels as a species of special concern, 139 nest boxes were placed throughout the state in 2006. As of 2014, more than 300 kestrel fledglings have been recorded and banded. **Ornithologists** hope these efforts will be enough to stabilize kestrel populations in the northeastern U.S.

Because the aplomado falcon is abundant today in Mexico and South America, it is not considered an endangered species. However, by the latter half of the 20th century, the aplomado falcon had been driven from the American Southwest by human interference. Its disappearance concerned raptor conservationists, so programs were established to reintroduce the species and provide nesting areas in its former habitats of Texas and

New Mexico. Since the 1990s, aplomado falcons have been successfully nesting in those states.

Everywhere falcons exist, they must compete with humans for resources. In places all around the world, logging, urban development, and agricultural expansion destroy trees that falcons need for nesting, and chemicals used for pest control cut off healthy food supplies. Continued research and conservation measures that aid falcons are vital to a future in which falcons fill the skies for generations to come.

*South America's aplomado falcon is named for its grayish plumage, as* aplomado *means "lead-colored" in Spanish.*

# ANIMAL TALE: FALCON AND COYOTE POPULATE THE EARTH

**Animal spirits are fundamental to the cultural history of the native peoples of the American West. The following myth from the Miwok people of California tells how the first birds and other animals were created to fill the earth with wildlife.**

---

Long ago, before there were humans or animals, only spirits existed. Two of these spirits, Falcon and Coyote, decided to fill the world with new life. "We need the feathers of Crow and Vulture," Coyote told Falcon. In those days, Crow had a long, beautiful tail, and Vulture had majestic head feathers.

"They will not share their feathers," Falcon said. "How can we get them?"

"With a trap," Coyote replied. He began to limp. "You see," he said with a smile, "I am dying."

Falcon laughed. "I will tell Crow and Vulture."

As Coyote limped through a meadow, Falcon flew to a tree where Crow was sunning himself. He called out, "Come see! Coyote is dying!"

"Coyote cannot die," Crow said. "He is a powerful spirit like us."

But Falcon persisted. "Look how he drags himself along. He won't last much longer."

Crow looked into the distance and saw Coyote looking very sickly. He flew down from his perch and headed for the meadow.

Then Falcon raced to the rock where Vulture was resting. "Come see!" Falcon called out. "Coyote is dying!"

"Coyote cannot die," Vulture said. "Like us, he is a powerful spirit."

"Look over there!" Falcon said. "He can barely move. He is near death."

Vulture squinted his eyes and looked toward the meadow. He was shocked to see Coyote lying on the ground, coughing. Immediately, Vulture flew toward the meadow. Falcon followed.

When Crow and Vulture reached Coyote, they found his motionless body on the ground. "He's dead!" they cried.

"Well then," said Falcon. "You should not waste him." And with that, he peeled back Coyote's fur to reveal a soft belly. Falcon smiled as Crow and Vulture began pecking at Coyote. They pecked until they had made a hole in Coyote's body. The greedy spirits then stepped inside the hole, and Falcon jumped inside with them. In a flash, Coyote leaped to his feet and pulled his fur around the spirits, trapping them inside his body.

Crow and Vulture panicked. It was dark, and as they fought to get out, Falcon gently plucked feathers from Crow's tail and Vulture's head. When he had gathered enough feathers, Falcon called out, "Coyote, please let us out!"

Coyote opened up his fur and freed the spirits. "Wasn't that a funny joke?" he asked.

"Hmm," said Crow, "not really."

"No," said Vulture, "not funny at all." And then the two spirits flew away, not even realizing that Crow no longer had a beautiful tail and Vulture no longer had head feathers.

Together, Falcon and Coyote planted the feathers in the ground, facing the four corners: north, south, east, and west. From the feathers sprang a multitude of creatures that looked exactly like Coyote and Falcon.

"This could be confusing," Falcon said to Coyote.

"You're right," Coyote replied. So Falcon and Coyote transformed many of the creatures into unique birds. They made the rest of the creatures into other animals. Then they instructed the new wildlife to fill the land and sea.

## GLOSSARY

**adaptability** – the ability to change to improve one's chances of survival in an environment

**carrion** – the rotting flesh of an animal

**coat of arms** – the official symbol of a family, state, nation, or other group

**contaminated** – negatively affected by exposure to a polluting substance

**cultural** – of or relating to particular groups in a society that share behaviors and characteristics that are accepted as normal by that group

**DDT** – a chemical compound used to kill pest insects that was later found to cause health problems in people who lived in environments where it was used

**endemic** – native to and confined to a certain geographical location

**evolved** – gradually developed into a new form

**extinction** – the act or process of becoming extinct; coming to an end or dying out

**feral** – in a wild state after having been domesticated

**glands** – organs in a human or animal body that produce chemical substances used by other parts of the body

**migrate** – to undertake a regular, seasonal journey from one place to another and then back again

**mythology** – a collection of myths, or popular, traditional beliefs or stories that explain how something came to be or that are associated with a person or object

**ornithologists** – scientists who study birds and their lives

**plumage** – the entire feathery covering of a bird

**steppes** – mostly treeless, dry, grassy plains characterized by extreme temperature changes from daytime to nighttime

**turbines** – machines that produce energy when wind or water spins through their blades, which are fitted on a wheel or rotor

**warm-blooded** – maintaining a relatively constant body temperature that is usually warmer than the surroundings

## SELECTED BIBLIOGRAPHY

Cornell Lab of Ornithology. "All About Birds: Peregrine Falcon." http://www.allaboutbirds.org/guide/peregrine_falcon/id.

Davis, Kate. *Falcons of North America*. Missoula, Mont.: Mountain Press, 2008.

Gallagher, Tim. *Falcon Fever: A Falconer in the Twenty-First Century*. Boston: Houghton Mifflin, 2008.

Minnesota Department of Natural Resources. "Prairie Falcon." http://www.dnr.state.mn.us/birds/prairiefalcon.html.

The Raptor Trust. "Falcons." http://theraptortrust.org/the -birds/hawk-facts/falcons/.

Wauer, Roland H. *The American Kestrel: Falcon of Many Names*. Boulder, Colo.: Johnson Books, 2005.

**Note:** Every effort has been made to ensure that any websites listed above were active at the time of publication. However, because of the nature of the Internet, it is impossible to guarantee that these sites will remain active indefinitely or that their contents will not be altered.

*American kestrels have longer wings in relation to their bodies than most other falcon species.*

## INDEX